100
CRI

ARCTURUS

With special thanks to Paul Lucas

ARCTURUS

This edition published in 2014 by Arcturus Publishing Limited
26/27 Bickels Yard, 151–153 Bermondsey Street,
London SE1 3HA

ISBN: 978-1-78212-283-8
AD003632UK

Printed in China

Contents

Introduction

Why is it that just when we most need to be creative, inspiration often deserts us? Is there some way to harness the imagination so that we can tap into it whenever we want to?

If you find yourself asking this question, then *1001 Ways to Creativity* is the book for you. Within its pages you'll find tips, tricks and inspirational examples to help unleash a stream of ideas whenever and wherever you really need them. Whether you are seeking

to become more creative in the arts or in the workplace, or are yearning to develop more creative relationships with your loved ones, this book will show you how to turn stale, tired thinking into new, fresh concepts. Brimming with insights into the creative process, it's a guide that will help you to slip into a creative state of mind, show you how to harness your imagination and, above all, demonstrate how to transform the ideas you generate into reality.

Forget the myth of the tortured genius waiting for the muse to visit: these days creativity is much too important to leave to chance.

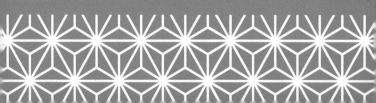

What is Creativity?

It is not something we can touch or capture, yet we all know what it is to feel creative. So what exactly is this mysterious force?

Creativity is a combination of talent and hard work. Most people have enough talent, but underestimate how much work is required.

Two little words can sum up creativity: 'What if?'

Creativity is not the finding of a thing, but the making something out of it after it is found.

James Russell Lowell

When curiosity is acted upon, it becomes creativity.

To be creative you must wander, and that means not being afraid to lose your way.

You learn creativity the same way you learn any skill: through practice.

Creativity is essentially a lonely art. An even lonelier struggle. To some a blessing. To others a curse. It is in reality the ability to reach inside yourself and drag forth from your very soul an idea.

Lou Dorfsman

Learn to trust your instincts. You will have to rely on them, rather than logic, to find true creativity.

To be creative you need a thin skin to feel the world, and a thick skin to protect you from the critics.

Creativity is a journey, not a destination.

One day we'll all find out that all of our songs were just little notes in a great big song.

Woody Guthrie

I believe there are two ways of writing novels. One is making a sort of musical comedy without music and ignoring real life altogether; the other is going deep down into life and not caring a damn. *P.G. Wodehouse*

All creativity stems, in the end, from your interaction with other people.

The creative person is an expert in having accidents.

At its best, creativity is inexplicable. Do not attempt to rationalize it, just go with the flow.

The entire universe was created out of nothing, and as yet no one has been able to logically explain how. The ultimate act of creativity is also the most mysterious.

The poet makes himself a seer by a long, prodigious, and rational disordering of all the senses. Every form of love, of suffering, of madness; he searches himself, he consumes all the poisons in him, and keeps only their quintessences.

Arthur Rimbaud

Nothing in the logical mind would look at a caterpillar and see the butterfly it will soon become.

Art has to move you and design does not, unless it's a good design for a bus.

David Hockney

There is no such thing as cautious creativity. Every creative act is daring.

Creativity is allowing yourself to make mistakes. Art is knowing which ones to keep.

Scott Adams

Everybody's recipe for creativity is different, but perseverance always features in the list of ingredients.

Don't tell me the moon is shining; show me the glint of light on broken glass.

Anton Chekhov

The only way into creativity is via the deep end.

Creativity does not run away from problems – it actively looks for them.

Creativity is not a thing, it is a way.

Working on our own consciousness is the most important thing that we are doing at any moment, and being love is a supreme creative act.

Ram Dass

There is no end to the creative process. Creativity is making a start, time and time again.

To be creative is to believe in life before death.

When what we expect to happen actually does happen, there is no creativity.

Creativity is knowing how to hide your sources.

Creative activity could be described as a type of learning process where teacher and pupil are located in the same individual.

Arthur Koestler

The straight and narrow is never the road to creativity.

Although you always have to leave your comfort zone in order to be creative, in the end creativity will leave you feeling truly in harmony with yourself for the first time.

The bait with which you will catch creativity is integrity.

Go further than you think you can.
That is where you will find creativity.

To draw, you must close your eyes and sing.

Pablo Picasso

New experiences fuel creativity: the more
you seek out new experiences the more
creative you are likely to become.

Creativity requires an extraordinary amount of faith mixed with just the right level of doubt.

The quickest way to become creative is to associate with creative people.

Creativity, as has been said, consists largely of rearranging what we know in order to find out what we do not know. Hence, to think creatively, we must be able to look afresh at what we normally take for granted.

George Kneller

Nobody is either 100 per cent creative or 100 per cent uncreative. Finding a way to mine your creative resources is the key to success.

A hunch is creativity trying
to tell you something.

This is the artist, then, life's hungry man, the glutton of eternity, beauty's miser, glory's slave.

Thomas Wolfe

You cannot force creativity – but you can and should create the conditions in which it will flourish.

Creativity decays when it is not used, and flows when it is regularly tapped.

The real voyage of discovery lies not in finding new lands, but in seeing with new eyes.

Marcel Proust

We are all born creative –
it is just that some of us
forget our creativity when
we leave childhood.

Creativity is always a question, never an answer.

True art takes note not merely of form but also of what lies behind.

Mahatma Gandhi

The creative person is the one who understands the rules but is not afraid to break them.

If you can identify what you most love and what you are most afraid of, you are most of the way towards becoming creative.

The greatest creative acts often flow forth from the tiniest details of life.

Anxiety is the handmaiden of creativity. *Chuck Jones*

Creativity transforms mistakes from barriers into springboards.

When you cease to accept things at face value, creativity follows.

To find creativity, first go in search of yourself.

We are all the children of Mother Nature's creativity. Evolution shaped every living thing through countless experiments, and human beings are just one of its latest field tests.

Creativity is thinking up new things. Innovation is doing new things.

Theodore Levitt

You can only learn how to swim in the pool of creativity by diving in.

The creative process is important even if it appears at first to produce nothing of value. Every honest attempt to create takes you one step closer to a creative triumph.

Creative ideas do not just produce great art – sometimes they produce great wealth too.

Creativity is intelligence having a day out.

A piece of art is never a finished work. It answers a question which has been asked, and asks a new question.

Robert Engman

Rediscovering is as creative as discovering.

The sworn enemy of creativity is common sense.

Everybody has creativity within them, and that includes you. To actually be creative, however, you must turn that inner creativity into action.

Creativity is 50 per cent inspiration and 50 per cent courage.

You can play without being creative, but you can't be creative without playing.

Art is when you hear a knocking from your soul — and you answer.

Terri Guillemets

Creativity grows from uncertainty.

Sometimes you have to break many boring rocks before you strike creative gold.

Imagination is more important than reality to the creative person, because it is often only through the imagination that we are able to find what is real.

As music is the poetry of sound, so is painting the poetry of sight.

James McNeill Whistler

Often we are at our most creative when we stop trying to be creative.

The world itself is incredibly creative, creating new material every day. All you have to do is to notice the changes and let them become your inspiration.

If there are limits to creativity, nobody has found them yet.

One of the greatest things about creativity is that it can turn brick walls into pathways, and obstacles into stepping stones.

A likely impossibility is always preferable to an unconvincing possibility. *Aristotle*

Creativity is a human need, just like food or water.

Creativity is what happens when you break free from habit.

You can trust that the creative process will be worth while, or you can believe that it will lead only to frustration and disappointment. Either way you will be right.

Chance is a creative force. Do not fear it: embrace it.

Creative work is not a selfish act or a bid for attention on the part of the actor. It's a gift to the world and every being in it. Don't cheat us of your contribution. Give us what you've got. *Steven Pressfield*

Creativity blurs the boundaries between the real and the imaginary.

The greatest work will be produced not when you manage to control your creativity, but when you allow your creativity to control you.

Inspiration is just dreary detail unless you have a creative outlook on life.

Creativity sometimes comes in sudden bursts when you least expect it, so you always need to be prepared to take advantage of such periods.

You invent your own definition of creativity every time you try something new.

If you had a million Shakespeares, could they write like a monkey? *Steven Wright*

Think of creativity as a spark it needs a large stockpile of experience to ignite. If you do not open yourself up to life then your creativity will just be a flash, and never a real fire.

Creativity has its head in the clouds – but its feet firmly on the ground.

Nothing worth while ever comes without serious effort, and this is particularly true with regards to creativity.

Art will remain the most astonishing activity of mankind born out of struggle between wisdom and madness, between dream and reality in our mind.

Magdalena Abakanowicz

Although creativity is difficult, it is rarely complicated. Rather it takes complicated notions and finds the simplicity within them.

You don't make creativity, you find it.

You are truly an artist if you can say that you would work even if you knew you would never receive any reward.

The most creative people you are likely to meet are children. If you want to know the essence of creativity then just observe them playing – that is the state that adults need to somehow find again.

Everything in the world is connected. Creativity is about finding connections where they are least expected.

Creative people know that there is no such thing as perfection – and that's okay.

The ability to ignore distractions is one of the key skills required to think creatively.

True storytelling reveals meaning without committing the error of defining it.

Hannah Arendt

Frustration kills creativity: relax, and allow your creative thoughts to flow.

Creativity is not in competition with anyone else or anything else – it is happy just to be what it is.

Not everything you try out will succeed, but all successful creative acts begin with trying something out.

Creativity is the blurred area where you end and the rest of the world begins.

This is the nature of genius, to be able to grasp the knowable even when no one else recognizes that it is present.

Deepak Chopra

Creativity is born from risk.

We tend to think of creativity in terms of frantic bursts of inspiration, but quiet reflection is also required to produce order from the chaos of the creative process.

We are all creative while asleep. Learn how to dream freely when you're awake, too.

Creative thinking is not a talent, it is a skill that can be learnt. It empowers people by adding strength to their natural abilities which improves teamwork, productivity and, where appropriate, profits.

Edward de Bono

Let the stillness speak to you, and the chaos too. Everything in your life has something to tell you, and creativity is the art of listening to all of life's voices.

Work harder, dream harder. Creativity requires both in large quantities.

When discipline and intelligence meet child-like play, creativity is born.

Art is a collaboration between God and the artist, and the less the artist does the better.

André Gide

You can only follow in the footsteps of others for so long. When you stop seeing the footsteps of others, you have reached the land of creativity.

Creativity is a struggle against nothingness.

Turn confusion into curiosity
and you are halfway to creativity.

Artists to my mind are the real architects of change, and not the political legislators who implement change after the fact.

William S. Burroughs

Set out to please nobody but yourself. You can't be creative if you are worried about what others will make of what you create.

A dream becomes a creative act only when it is acted upon.

Creativity is redefined by each new creative act. Go and create, and redefine it again.

Finding the Way

Once you learn to recognize creativity, you will rapidly realize that inspiration lies all around us.

In our day-to-day lives, we tend to overlook things rather than look at them. Make a conscious effort to pay attention to the very tiniest of details.

No creative person should ever be without a notepad and pencil.

Do at least one thing differently each day. Breaking patterns often releases creative thoughts.

When you're done for the day, try ending a piece of written work mid-sentence. That way, when you return to it you should find it easier to pick up where you left off.

Cut up old newspaper and magazine articles and rearrange the words. The new juxtapositions of familiar concepts can often spark the imagination.

The reason that art (writing, engaging, and all of it) is valuable is precisely why I can't tell you how to do it. If there were a map, there'd be no art, because art is the act of navigating without a map.

Seth Godin

There is something about walking which seems to spur creative thought. Whenever you have the option to walk, take it.

To steal ideas from one person is plagiarism; to steal from many is research.

In cafés or at bus stations, pick out a stranger and imagine a life story for them.

Don't think you have to be behind a desk to do creative work. Try working in a variety of environments to see what sparks creativity.

Be honest with yourself about when and where you are most creative, and make that time and space sacred.

Write it. Shoot it. Publish it. Crochet it, sauté it, whatever. MAKE.

Joss Whedon

When you lack inspiration, revisit something that has inspired you in the past and try to view it with new eyes.

Don't be discouraged when others tell you that their brilliance comes to them without any real effort. The vast majority of us have to work hard to find creativity.

Forget your failures, remember only your dreams.

Never imagine that an idea is too obvious, or stop because 'it must have been done before'. If you find your true voice then everything you create will be unique.

You can't wait for inspiration. Sometimes you have to go after it with a club.

Jack London

Try setting yourself strict deadlines if you find it hard to focus on creative projects.

Don't blame others for your frustrations. You can turn your frustrations into something creative if you are honest about them.

Get plenty of sleep. You may be on a roll creatively but that's of little use if you're too tired to function.

Team up with other creative people in your area or online. It really helps to be able to bounce ideas off other people.

Poetry and Hums aren't things which you get, they're things which get you. And all you can do is to go where they can find you.

A.A. Milne

Write what is in your head as soon as you get up in the morning. If you can remember your dreams, so much the better.

The more conservative your approach, the harder creativity becomes. Be daring!

Many people find that having music playing softly in the background helps their creativity. Experiment and see what works best for you.

Don't beat yourself up when progress is slow. Leave your work and return to it when you are feeling refreshed.

You need not even listen,
simply wait, just learn to
become quiet, and still,
and solitary. The world
will freely offer itself to
you to be unmasked. It
has no choice; it will roll
in ecstasy at your feet.

Franz Kafka

If everyone you knew was a cartoon super-hero, what would their special powers be? Make a list, and see if it sparks a creative project.

The truth will set you free – but not before it has really frustrated you.

Have you surprised yourself yet today? If the answer is no, what are you waiting for?

Letting go is an art. Practise daily.

You connect yourself to the viewer by sharing something that is inside of you that connects with something inside of him or her. All you have as your guide is that you know what moves you.

Steven Brust

Never throw away anything you have created. Even if you think it is not successful, it may spark new ideas if you return to it in the future.

Identifying false assumptions can be a great way to open the doors of creativity.

Your goal should be to learn more about yourself and your creative abilities each and every day.

Don't be afraid to show your work to others. Creative criticism is vitally important in helping you to improve your skills.

I don't wait for moods. You accomplish nothing if you do that. Your mind must know it has got to get down to work.

Pearl S. Buck

Set your own agenda. Just because others work in a particular way doesn't mean that way will work for you too.

In creative work,
you never get anywhere
interesting until you don't
know where you are.

**Begin anywhere, and at any time.
The important thing is to begin.**

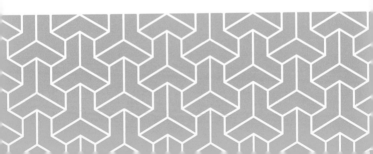

Your inner voice is often little more than a whisper. Don't let reason's shouts drown it out: an inkling is more valuable than a fact.

Anything done with love and enthusiasm is done well.

Take a trip to a museum or art gallery and study the techniques of the creative masters.

Get your hands dirty. Make a mess. Rejoice in the chaos of creativity.

Celebrate your creative works, and be proud of your achievements. Even if you are not happy with the results, you should congratulate yourself on being brave enough to try.

Nobody is 'a natural'. Those who think creativity should come easily are likely to give up when they are faced with confusion and doubt – and that's exactly when the process gets interesting.

Ideas only dry up when life dries up. It is always time to try a new experience.

Don't try to figure out what other people want to hear from you; figure out what you have to say. It's the one and only thing you have to offer.

Barbara Kingsolver

There are no short cuts to creativity.
But there are no dead ends either.

**You should never take
the creative process too
seriously. When you feel like
throwing something across
the room in frustration,
laugh at yourself instead.**

**If in doubt, make a cup of coffee.
Sometimes you just have to take a break.**

You don't need self-confidence to be creative, but you do need to believe that every human being is creative, including yourself.

Creativity is an action. How can you ever hope to experience creativity unless you actually try creating something?

At some point, you have to stop the creative process and declare your work finished. Endless tinkering in pursuit of perfection is futile.

You can't compare yourself to others. Compare your work to your own earlier works, and be honest about which aspects are better and which are worse.

Everyone is a creative genius when it comes to thinking up reasons not to try.

The infinite possibilities of the imagination can seem overwhelming at times. Just keep climbing, and don't look down.

If your expectations are too high then all you will create for yourself is frustration.

Don't feel inferior when you make mistakes. It is only by making lots of mistakes that you eventually become superior.

The creative mind plays
with the object it loves.
Carl Jung

Start with what seems obvious if you're
having trouble getting inspiration. Many
great ideas seem obvious in retrospect.

Sometimes you should
aim to deepen the mystery
rather than solve it.

One of the things I know about writing
is this: spend it all, shoot it, play it,
lose it, all, right away, every time. Do
not hoard what seems good for a later
place in the book or for another book;
give it, give it all, give it now.

Annie Dillard

Always be on the lookout for wonder.

When truly creative people come up with a new idea they don't reject it immediately because of its flaws. They play with it, looking for strengths and sliding over weaknesses.

David Campbell

Find the things that only you can say.

Don't aim to capture the feathers on a bird's wing: aim to capture the bird's flight.

Go and make interesting mistakes, make amazing mistakes, make glorious and fantastic mistakes. Break rules. Leave the world more interesting for your being here. Make. Good. Art.

Neil Gaiman

Try to express, not impress.

Organize your work space and keep it free from clutter. Often a messy working environment produces messy thinking.

The mind is like a parachute: it must be open to work.

Don't think about making art, just get it done. Let everyone else decide if it's good or bad, whether they love it or hate it. While they are deciding, make even more art.

Andy Warhol

The creative mind is always doing things for the very first time.

Don't neglect your sense of smell. It is the sense that most of us take for granted. Next time you go for a walk, try closing your eyes and blocking your ears for a moment and concentrating just on the smells.

Meditation can often be a useful way to get yourself into a creative mindset.

Every human being has hundreds of separate people living under his skin. The talent of a writer is his ability to give them their separate names, identities, and personalities and have them relate to other characters living with him.

Mel Brooks

Keep learning in order to inspire yourself. Take a class, or just study a new subject at home. All new knowledge brings new insight.

Look, take notes, and then look again. First impressions are sometimes spot on, but often looking at something for a second time reveals new details about your subject.

Reward yourself with little treats when you accomplish your creative goals.

You may not be a Picasso or Mozart but you don't have to be. Just create to create. Create to remind yourself you're still alive. Make stuff to inspire others to make something too. Create to learn a bit more about yourself.

Frederick Terral

Change your perspective. The view is different from every window in your house. Treat creative problems in a similar way, by looking at them from a variety of angles.

Take your worst fears and happiest dreams and spread them out on the table in front of you. Now you are ready to work.

Being creative means surfing the waves, not staring at the sea.

**Don't concentrate on how to have new and
original thoughts: concentrate on how to
remove the old and unoriginal ones.**

Think of everything
that happens to you
– good and bad –
as material.

All work and no play doesn't just make Jill and Jack dull, it kills the potential of discovery, mastery, and openness to change and flexibility and it hinders innovation and invention.

Joline Godfrey

Sometimes in order to create you must first have the courage to destroy.

Only those who risk going too far can possibly find out how far one can go.

T.S. Eliot

The only barriers to your creativity are those you build yourself.

Hold on to this thought: you can, and if you're brave enough, you will.

If in doubt, doodle.

To have a really good idea you need to have lots of ideas to choose from.

Originality doesn't mean saying what no one has ever said before, it just means speaking with a voice that no one has heard before – yours.

Learn to master your mind, not be mastered by your mind.

The bird of paradise alights only on the hand that does not grasp.

John Berry

As long as you are doing, you are doing it right.

Give attention to the details and the bigger picture will soon emerge.

All roads lead to nowhere if you don't know where you want to get to.

To be an artist you have to give up everything, including the desire to be a good artist.

Jasper Johns

Learn to see the statue that lurks within the block of marble.

Do what you can rather than dwelling on what you can't.

There are always flowers for those who want to see them.

Henri Matisse

Chaotic doing can be more creative than orderly thinking.

If you're having problems starting a piece of written work, try writing the end of your piece and working backwards from there.

Use word associations to unlock
your subconscious. Write a subject
and then think of the first word that
you associate with that subject.
Then think of what you associate
with that word, and so on.

I dream a lot. I do more painting when I'm not painting. It's in the subconscious.

Andrew Wyeth

Inspiration arrives unexpectedly – but only comes to the well-prepared mind.

Every idea seems crazy at first.

The earth has music for those who listen.

William Shakespeare

A small step now will always take you further than a big step in the future.

Talk to yourself. Take opposite sides in an inner argument. It doesn't matter who wins – it is the dialogue that matters.

Incorporate chance into your decision-making. Throw a dice, or toss a coin, to decide what happens next.

When the imagination
fails you, turn to
memories for inspiration.

**To find creativity,
lose your fear of
being wrong.**

Believe in yourself: everything else flows from that.

The main thing is to be moved, to love, to hope, to tremble, to live.

Auguste Rodin

Creativity is always beginning, and is never truly finished.

Doing dreary work like cleaning or ironing can sometimes allow your mind to wander freely and produce creative thoughts.

Be a tourist for a day in your home town. Visit a regular haunt as if you were collecting information for a tourist guide. By looking at familiar places with different eyes you begin to see anew.

Take a trip to a cemetery. Pick a name from a headstone, and imagine a life for that person.

Art reaches its greatest peak when devoid of self-consciousness. Freedom discovers man the moment he loses concern over what impression he is making or about to make.

Bruce Lee

Dream, don't plan.

Make a prediction as to what will happen the following day. When you return to your prediction, note not whether it came true or not, but what assumptions you based your forecast on. It's these assumptions that we need to challenge in order to become creative.

Focus on being in a creative state rather than making something creative. Once you feel creative, the making is relatively easy.

Force yourself to generate as many ideas as possible in under 10 minutes. Don't worry about how crazy or illogical the ideas are – just let them flow. Later on, pick one or two of the best and see where they take you.

Do not be troubled
for a language,
cultivate your soul
and she will show
herself. *Eugène Delacroix*

**Slow down. Remind yourself to do
everyday things more slowly so that
you can pay more attention to them,
and see for the first time what you
usually take for granted.**

Learn to take criticism. Few creative works are perfect, and often a second pair of eyes can spot flaws that the creator missed.

Often a great idea begins with a silly question.

You must be creative enough to find the time and space for your creativity.

The Creative Heart

How can we develop more
creative relationships and
allow our hearts to guide us
down new and exciting paths?

The only part of you
that can live forever
is your heart –
and the way it lives
is through the works
you create.

Art is literacy of the heart.

Elliot Eisner

To become truly creative you must first learn to put aside your ego.

The reason the heart is so important to creative work is because all originality comes from honesty.

The questions that the heart asks are always more universal than those the mind asks.

If I create from the heart, nearly everything works; if from the head, almost nothing.

Marc Chagall

A broken heart can produce as much creativity, if not more, than a heart which has never known pain.

What you create with your heart will touch the hearts of others. That which you don't, won't.

If you don't fully embrace your ideas then they'll never come to fruition: be a brave heart.

If creativity were just about logic, computers would have taken over from human beings by now.

In fact, everything we encounter in this world with our six senses is an inkblot test. You see what you are thinking and feeling, seldom what you are looking at.

Shiqin

How does it feel to feel? Creative.

The heart is what keeps us in contact with nature. We connect to the rest of the living world through empathy and compassion. If that bond ever becomes broken it is almost impossible to create anything meaningful.

**Wear your heart on your sleeve –
and dip your pen in it to create.**

In every man's heart
there is a secret nerve
that answers to the
vibration of beauty.

Christopher Morley

**The heart is sometimes quiet,
but never silent.**

The mind serves us well when we need to find the sensible solution to a problem.
In creative matters, however, it is always the heart that leads us in the right direction.

Faint heart never won fair creativity.

Whenever we have a change of heart, the world changes slightly too.

The biggest mistake any creative person can ever make is to express what they think they should feel, rather than what they really do feel.

If you feel like laughing and crying at the same time, then you are probably on the right lines.

One of the best ways to relax is to concentrate solely on the beat of your heart. In this way the heart can relax the mind, throwing open the doors of creativity.

You cannot fake creativity. If you are not prepared to work from your heart then you may as well give up.

The heart is never self-conscious. If you learn to trust your heart you will soon find that you create freely.

The most creative gift you have to offer the world is your life.

All mankind's inner feelings eventually manifest themselves as an outer reality.

Stuart Wilde

To be heartless
is to be artless.

Use your mind and
your senses for the
finer details, and use
your heart to see the
bigger picture.

Fall in love with creativity and it will fall in love with you too.

The heart has mountains and valleys, just as the world has. Don't be afraid to explore both the highs and the lows, in both your heart and the world.

Every portrait that is painted with feeling is a portrait of the artist, not of the sitter.

Oscar Wilde

Make sure your inner world is a happy place to be. Without it, you are simply a puppet of your surroundings.

The heart knows what it wants to say; the problem is silencing the mind so that you can hear clearly.

The experiences in life that make the heart beat faster are usually the same ones that create great art.

To be creative you must feel creative, not think creative.

The heart is a muscle that needs exercising like any other muscle.

The most enduring relationships are often cultivated through collaboration in creative projects.

What is creativity if not freedom? How can you feel truly free unless all of you is free – mind, body and spirit?

It is only with the heart that one can see rightly; what is essential is invisible to the eye.

Antoine de Saint-Exupéry

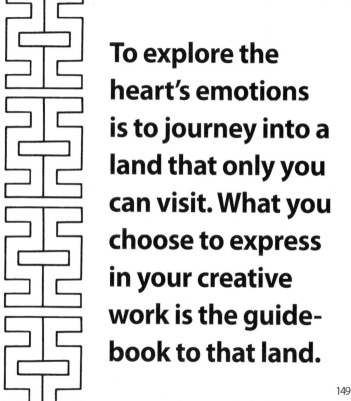

To explore the heart's emotions is to journey into a land that only you can visit. What you choose to express in your creative work is the guidebook to that land.

149

We all tend to spend our time trying to blend in and conform, so as not to be thought of as 'weird' or 'different'. When attempting to create, however, we must be as weird and different as possible.

An enthusiastic heart is the best protection against the disappointments that inevitably face the creative worker.

Creativity is what happens when the heart melts.

Much of the very best creative work flows from the struggle between the heart and the mind.

Evolution and all hopes for a better world rest in the fearlessness and open-hearted vision of people who embrace life.

John Lennon

The inner child is the adult heart asking for permission to play.

The mind can only deal with the possible. To tackle the impossible worlds of the imagination you need to use your heart.

There are already millions of creative works in the world, so why should you add to that stockpile? The truth is that creativity is not rational – it is a yearning that comes from the heart.

Be like the Tin Man in The Wizard of Oz:
go in search of your heart.

Creativity is the battle to give eloquence to the mumblings of the heart.

The act of painting is about
one heart telling another heart
where he found salvation.

Francisco Goya

The triumphs and disasters of falling in and out of love are the ultimate source of creative material.

That which is heart-felt is never wrong.

Make a conscious effort to question what you feel, and why.

Nothing you create will ever be real unless your heart is true.

Fill your paper with the breathings of your heart.

William Wordsworth

What is logical about the hundreds of hours that Michelangelo spent painting the ceiling of the Sistine Chapel?

Creativity requires unpredictability, and nothing is more unpredictable than the human heart.

Diligent research provides the fuel for creative work, but it is always the heart that ignites that fuel.

All genius paints with the pigment of emotion.

No heart is entirely light or entirely dark – and no great piece of art is either.

It is the individual who is not interested in his fellow men who has the greatest difficulties in life and provides the greatest injury to others.

Alfred Adler

Why should a vase be an art object, but not your life?

Having a great feeling about a project is often more important than having a great idea.

**Great scientists think clearly.
Great artists feel clearly.**

Just as we rarely use all of our brain's potential, so many of us rarely use all of our heart's potential.

The only restraints on the heart are those imposed by the mind.

Your success in being creative is entirely dependent upon the strength of your desire.

You cannot touch the hearts of others unless you yourself are able to laugh, and to cry.

We can never truly understand our feelings, but creativity illuminates them for us in new ways.

Expanding the mind means expanding the heart too.

Work for a cause, not for applause.

Art must be an expression of love or it is nothing.

Marc Chagall

The feelings that take you by surprise are the ones that are the most rewarding to explore.

When the conscious mind
feels alone in the universe,
it is creativity that restores
a sense of oneness.

Our brains teem with thoughts and ideas that we are totally unaware of. It is the heart that plucks these jewels from the subconscious and brings them to our attention.

Creative works often seem perfectly rational in hindsight, but are rarely produced through purely rational processes.

Don't just 'brainstorm', allow yourself to get soaked in the occasional 'heartstorm' too.

A moment's insight is more valuable
than a lifetime of looking but not seeing.

Art attracts us only by what it reveals of our most secret self.

Jean-Luc Godard

Don't accept everything that your heart says at face value. Analyse your instincts objectively – sometimes they are nothing more than prejudices.

The more you feel, the more you will create.

Write with your heart –
and then rewrite with your head.

We create precisely because we do not know everything.

The muscles of writing are not so visible, but they are just as powerful: determination, attention, curiosity, a passionate heart.
Natalie Goldberg

All ideas are fragile when they are first born. Be gentle with them, and nurture them until they are able to stand on their own two feet.

Creative desire needs to be kindled, and then regularly fuelled.

Give your love freely, and love will come back to you. The experience will enrich your life, and your work.

The brain relies on the logic of a past and a future. The heart, by contrast, beats constantly in the present.

One of the most creative acts you can perform is to encourage and inspire others in their creative endeavours.

The heart is forever young, so consult it whenever the body tires.

Anything that is begun in a half-hearted fashion will end up being half-baked when it is finished.

We describe certain experiences as 'moving': creativity takes that movement and turns it into a journey.

Being an author is having angels whisper in your ear – and devils, too.

Graycie Harmon

Don't just learn
new things – feel
new things too.

**Every creative act is an
attempt to put another piece
of the jigsaw of life in place.**

Not only are two heads better than one, but two hearts are better than one as well.

You will know you have created a successful work when your heart swells with pride.

I like to think of psychic energy as akin to radio waves. Even without the radio on, the air is filled with invisible signals from countless radio stations operating on their various frequencies. All you have to do to receive them is to flick the radio on and tune the dial.

John Edward

Fall truly, madly, deeply in love with creativity.

There is no such thing as objective reality: we all shape reality subjectively with our hearts.

The creative heart treats every experience the world offers as a gift.

Do not be afraid of the dark corners of your heart: they sometimes produce the richest creative works.

You will truly be living the dream when you dream for a living.

We can only be said to be alive in those moments when our hearts are conscious of our treasures.

Thornton Wilder

One of the greatest wonders in the world is the fact that we can wonder in the first place.

The heart is not a single voice, but a choir of voices: listen carefully.

They say that children should be seen but not heard. The inner child can't be seen, but needs to be heard.

Only passions, and great passions, can raise the soul to great things. Without them there is no sublimity, either in morals or in creativity. Art returns to infancy and virtue becomes small-minded.

Denis Diderot

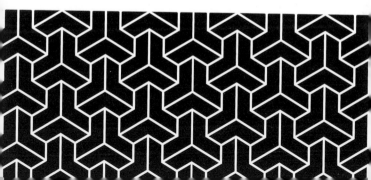

Just as a large percentage of your life is spent dreaming, so a large percentage of your creativity should come from dreams.

A change of heart is often exactly what you need to find the right direction.

You need to feel truly at home with creativity in order to produce great works – and we all know that home is where the heart is.

There's a reason why when we know something inside out and back to front, we describe it as knowing 'by heart'.

When we speak the word 'life', it must be understood we are not referring to life as we know it from its surface of fact, but to that fragile, fluctuating centre which forms never reach.

Antonin Artaud

The heart is a magpie that steals things without us noticing it has done so. Look into the nest and you might be dazzled by what is there.

How do we create something from nothing? With desire.

Consuming creative works with your heart is just as important as creating them with your heart.

Without creativity the heart can never be free.

Be angry, be sad, be happy, be crazy, be whatever you like – but always be passionately so.

Creativity is what spills out when your heart overflows.

Never, ever lose heart.

Working Creatively

It is often in the workplace that we feel least inspired – but a creative outlook can boost our productivity and bring a sense of fulfilment to our work.

When you work with your imagination, your office can be a palace and you can commute there on a flying carpet.

I have no taste for either poverty or honest labor, so writing is the only recourse left for me.

Hunter S. Thompson

In a creative team, every member of the team needs to be a leader. Simply following others is not creativity.

If you are not a hard taskmaster to yourself, you will never reach your true creative potential.

Forget any thoughts of effortlessly knocking out creative works while reclining in the sunshine: creativity is born from blood, sweat and tears.

Don't litter your workspace with keepsakes and reminders. A clutter-free environment is generally the most productive type of environment.

A lot of creative people find that setting daily targets helps to motivate them.

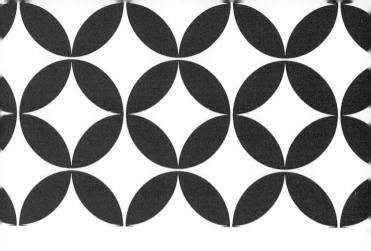

It is necessary to work, if not from inclination, at least from despair. Everything considered, work is less boring than amusing oneself.

Charles Baudelaire

Often a work project seems uninspiring because it is too familiar. Turn dull tasks into creative tasks by challenging yourself to do better than you did last time.

If you only create when you are 'in the mood' you will create very little.

If things don't seem to be flowing, switch your attention to a different project by all means – but don't simply give up and stop trying.

Take a trip to the sea or the mountains. Put things in perspective before you begin work and you will find your work seems far less arduous.

Nothing is more satisfying than admiring a work you have created after a particularly difficult struggle.

Art is not about thinking something up. It is the opposite – getting something down.

Julia Cameron

At work, everyone tends to become dull and predictable due to the repetitive nature of the daily routine. Talk to others about their lives outside work and you soon find they become more animated and inspired. If you can tap into that mindset, creativity will flow more easily.

As you become more used to creative work, it should get easier and easier – so keep practising.

There is no better feeling than creating. To get to the point where ideas are flowing freely, however, can often be difficult and exhausting work.

Creativity is not a pool that you gradually drain – it is more like a muscle which grows stronger the more often it is exercised.

Work will always be with us, and many works are worthy. But the worthiest works of all often reflect an artful creativity that looks more like play than work.

James Ogilvy

In terms of fame and riches, you don't always get what you deserve. In terms of the quality of your creative output, however, you get out exactly what you put in.

Trying to control everything only leads to frustration and predictability. Learn how to let go – of yourself and of your desire to control others.

As a creative person, your line manager is your own heart.

Almost anyone can be an author; the business is to collect money and fame from this state of being.

A.A. Milne

Check your posture to make sure you are in a comfortable position while working. Creative work takes enough out of the mind and soul without the body suffering too.

If you're trying to work creatively at a computer, close all programs that do not relate to your work. It is easy to get distracted by checking emails, social network contacts and so on.

When you can't tell the difference between working and playing, you will know that you have mastered the art of creativity.

I love being a writer. What I can't stand is the paperwork.

Peter De Vries

Take your watch off, and remove all clocks from the room you are working in. You need to immerse yourself in the present in order to be creative.

As long as you have inspiration, you will never be out of work, creatively speaking.

If you start to feel frustrated, take a break. Work, but don't get worked up.

There's no retirement for an artist, it's your way of living so there's no end to it.

Henry Moore

To create like a god you must first work like a slave.

Often you will have to fit creative work around your day job. That is not a problem – as long as you treat turning up late to either job as an equally serious matter.

If an idea is too fragile to survive being bounced around, then it wasn't a very good idea.

When it is working, you completely go into another place, you're tapping into things that are totally universal, completely beyond your ego and your own self. That's what it's all about.

Keith Haring

A calm mind usually achieves more than one that is full of wild and unfocused ideas.

We are what we repeatedly do. Excellence, then, is not an act but a habit.

Aristotle

The commute to and from work can be the most inspirational part of the working day if your mind is tuned to think creatively.

Nobody ever got to work wonders without serving a long apprenticeship working their tail off first.

We all know the experience of 'just needing to get the job done'. At such times, creative approaches can seem like a luxury we can ill afford – but in actual fact the imaginative path often takes us where we need to go more quickly than the obvious path.

The world is constantly changing. A workspace with a window will provide an infinite amount of fresh inspiration.

Any fool can paint a picture, but it takes a wise person to be able to sell it.

Samuel Butler

The way to tackle most creative problems is to work through them until they become creative opportunities.

Finding your own way of working is perhaps the most important part of the creative process.

The Muse is like a talented but unreliable employee. Make sure she knows who's boss.

The creative worker needs talent, but talent is of no value without work.

Although there are many legends of artists who worked best while drunk, as a general rule you should avoid alcohol when working creatively. Get drunk on inspiration instead.

Regular breaks will help you to stay fresh and focused.

We can all be guilty of taking work problems home with us. Since creative work often takes place in the home, it is especially important that you find a way to deal with the many frustrations the creative process throws up.

Without a proper work/life balance, you will never feel whole enough to be creative.

Difficult tasks can be completed with hard work alone, but miracles require creativity.

I am interested in art as a means of living a life; not as a means of making a living.

Robert Henri

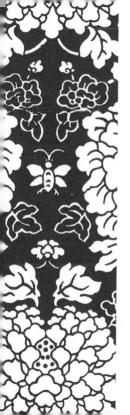

All work and no play makes Jack a dull boy – and makes Jack create dull works too.

The true domain of the creative worker is the inner world, no matter where they happen to be working.

Try taking a creative holiday to find inspiration. Go somewhere new, but take all your creative tools with you, and resolve to work during your break rather than lounging on a beach.

Through creativity you can promote yourself from a serf to the ruler of a kingdom.

Creative cats have to work like dogs.

Creativity means being
The New Guy or Gal every day.

When I work, I work very fast, but preparing to work can take any length of time.

Cy Twombly

All creative people work in the laboratory of the human heart.

Makers don't waste their time making money.

Lots of people work hard and play hard – but only creative people get to do both at the same time.

The
Spirit of
Creativity

To become truly creative we must connect deeply with the world, and with our inner selves. This section explores how we might look within for inspiration, rather than seeking it in the outside world.

The real meaning of life is to create something that makes the world a better place to be.

No bird soars too high, if he soars with his own wings.

William Blake

Think of all the beauty that creative people have brought into the world. Now imagine how much more beauty is just waiting to be born.

Everyone needs something to believe in. Creative people believe in the transformative power of their imagination, and the imaginations of others.

Nothing is more damaging to creativity than received wisdom.

To me, the greatest pleasure of writing is not what it's about, but the inner music the words make.

Truman Capote

The ability to appreciate the beauty of creativity is what makes humans unique in the world.

The soul should always stand ajar, ready to welcome the ecstatic experience.

Emily Dickinson

There are no hard and fast rules when it comes to creativity. That is why you must rely on your spirit, rather than your mind, in order to create.

No matter who or where we are, we are all only one dream away from paradise.

The world is a canvas upon which we paint with our imaginations.

If you touch one thing with deep awareness, you touch everything.

Thích Nhất Hạnh

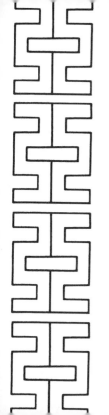

The creative spirit
is what moves
us when we see
the first flower of
spring.

Construction happens
because something useful
is needed; creation happens
because something that is
loved does not yet exist.

233

If we lived forever we might well not have the urge to create. But we don't, and the urge will never go away, so make a start today.

The day came when the risk to remain tight in a bud was more painful than the risk it took to blossom.

Anaïs Nin

Humans are part animal, part angel. Creativity is our attempt to reach for the stars.

Better keep yourself clean and bright.
You are the window through which
you must see the world.

George Bernard Shaw

Creativity is a hopeful message in a bottle that we cast on the seas of time.

Having the vision to see far is one thing, but going to the places you see is quite another.

Very few people look back on their lives and wish they had used their creativity less.

All true artists, whether they know it or not, create from a place of no-mind, from inner stillness.

Eckhart Tolle

The spirit cannot soar if it is weighed down by doubt. Have faith, and see where it leads you.

Creativity lies within all of us. The trick is to learn how to open ourselves up in order to discover what is already there.

Human beings were creating cave art at least 40,000 years ago – and we have probably been creating one type of art or another for as long as we have been human beings. Creativity is what defines us as a species.

I've never believed in God, but I believe in Picasso.

Diego Rivera

There is no such thing as absolute creative success or absolute creative failure. Aim to truly satisfy your creative impulses and if you achieve that then the process will have been worth while.

The prophets of all the world's great religions had one thing in common: they were all creative.

Nothing in science explains why we are so moved by the sight of a beautiful sunset.

Adventure is not outside a man, it is within.

David Grayson

Always aim high, as it is better to fall short than to aim too low in the first place.

Creativity is the thread that connects us to the eternal.

We do not know what tomorrow will bring. That can be frightening to some, but to the creative person it is intensely liberating.

Let the beauty we love be what we do. There are hundreds of ways to kneel and kiss the ground. *Rumi*

The only real journey
that we ever take in life is
within ourselves.

**How does it feel to be
you, right now? That is the
question your creative
work should try to answer.**

Giving praise to creativity is also a creative act.

The true work of art is but a shadow of the divine perfection.

Michelangelo

Just as children cannot seem to walk around puddles, so the creative person cannot pass by an opportunity to create.

We change every day, whether we wish to or not, so embrace that change and shape it to create the person you really want to become.

Nothing that can be bought is remotely as valuable as your imagination.

Like water which can clearly mirror the sky and the trees only so long as its surface is undisturbed, the mind can only reflect the true image of the Self when it is tranquil and wholly relaxed.

Indra Devi

Your body wakes each morning automatically, but make sure your imagination wakes up at the same time.

Just as every snowflake is slightly different, so is every creative act.

To be creative is to write a guidebook for a destination that exists only in your imagination.

The life which is not examined is not worth living.

Plato

Put your ear close to your soul and listen to its whispers.

You are what you create.

Have no expectations when you enter the creative realm. Do not think of what you should do, or even what you could do, just be open and trusting and see what emerges from within.

Every artist dips his brush in his own soul, and paints his own nature into his pictures.

Henry Ward Beecher

Nothing epitomizes the spirit of creativity more than man's first steps on the moon.

Only the person with a creative soul can see the universe in a grain of sand.

The spirit needs to rest from time to time, just as the body does. Creativity emerges from contrasts – the stars would not shine without the darkness.

The reward of art is not fame or success but intoxication.

Cyril Connolly

It is only through doing that the spirit is released: what is the point of building beautiful dream castles if no one can ever visit them?

Creative work doesn't just represent something, it is something; a living creation in its own right.

O great creator of being, grant us one more hour to perform our art and perfect our lives.

Jim Morrison

In the right hands, every pen and paint brush is a magic wand.

Think of how much the world has changed since you were a child. Who would have believed that so much change was possible? Who can predict what changes the future will bring? One thing we do know: the creative people will be the ones who make and shape the changes that affect us all.

An artist chooses his subjects. That is the way he praises.

Friedrich Nietzsche

We are all unique products of evolution by natural selection. Nature is the ultimate creative force, the ultimate creative spirit.

The spirit is not perfect; it makes mistakes. Often these mistakes lead us on our greatest creative journeys.

To conform is to cage the spirit, and
a caged spirit creates only problems.
To create happiness for yourself
and others, set your spirit free.

The man who has no
imagination has no wings.
Muhammad Ali

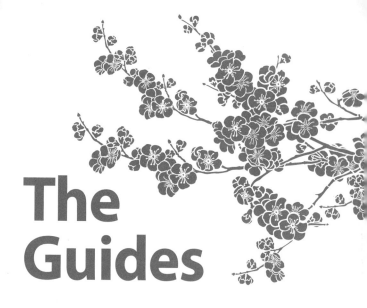

The
Guides

Words of wisdom from those who have
gone in search of creativity – sometimes
successfully and sometimes in vain.

There is no greater agony than bearing an untold story inside you.

Maya Angelou

Our society is run by insane people for insane objectives. I think we're being run by maniacs for maniacal ends and I think I'm liable to be put away as insane for expressing that. That's what's insane about it.

John Lennon

All human development, no matter what form it takes, must be outside the rules; otherwise we would never have anything new.

Charles Kettering

The uncreative mind can spot wrong answers, but it takes a very creative mind to spot wrong questions.

Antony Jay

A fine thought in fine language is a most precious jewel, and should not be hid away, but be exposed for use and ornament.

Arthur Conan Doyle

Better to write for yourself and have no public than to write for the public and have no self.

Cyril Connolly

If it adapts itself to what the majority of our society wants, art will be a meaningless recreation.

Albert Camus

We shall not cease from exploration,
and at the end of all our exploring
will be to arrive where we started and
know the place for the first time.

T.S. Eliot

The art of creation is older than the art of killing.

Andrei Voznesensky

Play so that you may be serious.

Anacharsis

I am a writer who came from a sheltered life. A sheltered life can be daring as well. For all serious daring starts from within.

Eudora Welty

Either write something worth reading or do something worth writing.

Benjamin Franklin

At moments of great enthusiasm it seems to me that no one in the world has ever made something this beautiful and important.

M.C. Escher

We are all apprentices in a craft where no one ever becomes a master.

Ernest Hemingway

Musical comedies aren't written, they are rewritten.

Stephen Sondheim

It is our choices that show what we truly are, far more than our abilities.

J.K. Rowling

The life of the creative man is led, directed and controlled by boredom. Avoiding boredom is one of our most important purposes.

Saul Steinberg

Primitives of our own species, even today, are historically shallow in their knowledge of the past. Only the poet who writes speaks his message across the millennia to other hearts.

Loren Eiseley

Imagination is the beginning of creation.

George Bernard Shaw

Writers are not just people who sit down and write. They hazard themselves. Every time you compose a book your composition of yourself is at stake. ***E.L. Doctorow***

Great things are not accomplished by those who yield to trends and fads and popular opinion.

Jack Kerouac

The writer writes in order to teach himself, to understand himself, to satisfy himself; the publishing of his ideas, though it brings gratification, is a curious anticlimax.

Alfred Kazin

The best style is the style you don't notice.

W. Somerset Maugham

Do not be satisfied with the stories that come before you. Unfold your own myth.

Rumi

One must be drenched in words, literally soaked in them, to have the right ones form themselves into the proper pattern at the right moment.

Hart Crane

Necessity is the mother of invention, it is true – but its father is creativity, and knowledge is the midwife.

Jonathan Schattke

Writing is both mask and unveiling.

E.B. White

There is no doubt that creativity is the most important human resource of all. Without creativity, there would be no progress, and we would be forever repeating the same patterns.

Edward de Bono

Congratulate yourselves if you have done something strange and extravagant and broken the monotony of a decorous age.

Ralph Waldo Emerson

The skill of writing is to create a context in which other people can think.

Edwin Schlossberg

Art is a marriage of the conscious and the unconscious.

Jean Cocteau

Might we not say that every child at play behaves like a creative writer, in that he creates a world of his own, or, rather, rearranges the things of his world in a new way which pleases him?

Sigmund Freud

An author is one who can judge his own stuff's worth, without pity, and destroy most of it.

Colette

Life isn't about finding yourself.
Life is about creating yourself.
George Bernard Shaw

**If you can see your path laid
out in front of you step by
step, you know it's not your
path. Your own path you
make with every step you
take. That's why it's your path.**

Joseph Campbell

No artist tolerates reality.

Friedrich Nietzsche

Great art picks up where nature ends.

Marc Chagall

I write because I like to make things and the only things I am good at making things with are words.

P.J. O'Rourke

There are only two ways of telling the complete truth - anonymously and posthumously. *Thomas Sowell*

Drama, instead of telling us the whole of a man's life, must place him in such a situation, tie such a knot, that when it is untied, the whole man is visible.

Leo Tolstoy

Fiction is the truth inside the lie. *Stephen King*

There is no escape from you. The only way out is in.

Spike Milligan

The process of writing has something infinite about it. Even though it is interrupted each night, it is one single notation.

Elias Canetti

Believe those who are seeking the truth. Doubt those who find it.

André Gide

How vain it is to sit down to write when you have not stood up to live.

Henry David Thoreau

The day is coming when a single carrot, freshly observed, will set off a revolution.

Paul Cézanne

I'd rather be caught holding up
a bank than stealing so much as a
two-word phrase from another writer.

Jack Smith

**Inspiration could be called inhaling the
memory of an act never experienced.**

Ned Rorem

Words are things. A small drop of ink, falling like dew upon a thought, produces that which makes thousands, perhaps millions, think.

Lord Byron

Art is not what you see, but what you make others see.

Edgar Degas

Have your adventures, make your mistakes, and choose your friends poorly – all these make for great stories.

Chuck Palahniuk

Imagination is the one weapon in the war against reality.

Jules de Gaultier

You don't have to burn books to destroy a culture. Just get people to stop reading them.

Ray Bradbury

We do not write as we want, but as we can.

W. Somerset Maugham

A little talent is good to have if you want to be a writer, but the only real requirement is the ability to remember every scar.

Stephen King

Writing gives you the illusion of control, and then you realize it's just an illusion, that people are going to bring their own stuff into it.

David Sedaris

Genius is 1 per cent inspiration, and 99 per cent perspiration.

Thomas Edison

Writing comes more easily if you have something to say.

Sholem Asch

The mind which plunges into Surrealism, relives with burning excitement the best part of childhood.

André Breton

Figuring out our gifts in life is part of our journey to becoming enlightened human beings. *Allison DuBois*

Resist much. Obey little.

Walt Whitman

We work in the dark, we give what we have. Our doubt is our passion, and our passion is our task. The rest is the madness of art.

Henry James

The writer, when he is also an artist, is someone who admits what others don't dare reveal.

Elia Kazan

A classic is classic not because it conforms to certain structural rules, or fits certain definitions . . . It is classic because of a certain eternal and irrepressible freshness.

Edith Wharton

It's much more important to write than to be written about.

Gabriel García Márquez

Every author in some way portrays himself in his works, even if it be against his will.

Goethe

If a true artist were born in a pigpen and raised in a sty, he would still find plenty of inspiration for his work. The only need is the eye to see.

Willa Cather

The artist is a receptacle for emotions that come from all over the place: from the sky, from the earth, from a scrap of paper, from a passing shape, from a spider's web.

Pablo Picasso

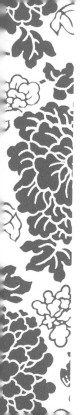

I was reading the dictionary. I thought it was a poem about everything.

Steven Wright

Like most – maybe all – writers, I learned to write by writing and, by example, by reading books.

Francine Prose

No one has ever written, painted, sculpted, modelled, built or invented except literally to get out of hell.

Antonin Artaud

Without inspiration the best powers of the mind remain dormant. There is a fuel in us which needs to be ignited with sparks.

Johann Gottfried von Herder

The object isn't to make art, it's to be in that wonderful state which makes art inevitable.

Robert Henri

The difference between the man who just cuts lawns and a real gardener is in the touching ... The lawn-cutter might just as well not have been there at all; the gardener will be there a lifetime.

Ray Bradbury

I will be an artist or nothing!

Eugene O'Neill

Life is infinitely stranger than anything which the mind of man could invent.

Arthur Conan Doyle

I'm painting an idea, not an ideal. Basically I'm trying to paint a structured painting full of controlled, and therefore potent, emotion.

Euan Uglow

The most beautiful thing we can experience is the mysterious. It is the source of all true art and science.

Albert Einstein

Life is the art of drawing without an eraser.

John W. Gardner

At some point in life the world's beauty becomes enough. You don't need to photograph, paint, or even remember it. It is enough.

Toni Morrison

What is life, but a series of inspired follies?

George Bernard Shaw

The writer, like everyone else, is equipped in infancy with a thick padding of things he believes to be true, but which aren't.

Jon Franklin

Personality is everything in art and poetry.

Goethe

Are we to paint what's on the face, what's inside the face, or what's behind it?

Pablo Picasso

Don't worry about people stealing your ideas. If your ideas are any good, you'll have to ram them down people's throats.

Howard Aiken

I write only because
There is a voice within me
That will not be still.

Sylvia Plath

If you do not expect the unexpected
you will not find it, for it is not to be
reached by search or trail.

Heraclitus

The good ideas are all hammered out in agony by individuals, not spewed out by groups.

Charles Brower

The joy is in creating, not maintaining.

Vince Lombardi

Stuff your eyes with wonder, live as if you'd drop dead in ten seconds. See the world. It's more fantastic than any dream made or paid for in factories.

Ray Bradbury

Follow your inner moonlight; don't hide the madness.

Allen Ginsberg

God spare me sclerosis of the curiosity, for the curiosity which craves to keep us informed about the small things no less than the large is the mainspring, the dynamo, the jet propulsion of all complete living.

John Brown

To create one's world in any of the arts takes courage.

Georgia O'Keeffe

A sincere artist is not one who makes a faithful attempt to put on to canvas what is in front of him, but one who tries to create something which is, in itself, a living thing.

William Dobell

Talent hits a target no one else can hit; Genius hits a target no one else can see.

Arthur Schopenhauer

If you can't play all the instruments in the orchestra of story, no matter what music may be in your imagination, you're condemned to hum the same old tune.

Robert McKee

It is good to have an end to journey toward; but it is the journey that matters, in the end.

Ursula Le Guin

No matter how old you get, if you can keep the desire to be creative, you're keeping the man-child alive.

John Cassavetes

Creative novelty springs largely from the rearrangement of the existing knowledge, a rearrangement that is itself an addition to knowledge.

J. Kneller

Style is knowing who you are, what you want to say, and not giving a damn.

Gore Vidal

In the creative state a man is taken out of himself. He lets down as it were a bucket into his subconscious, and draws up something which is normally beyond his reach. He mixes this thing with his normal experiences and out of the mixture he makes a work of art.

E.M. Forster

Talent is God-given. Be humble.
Fame is man-given. Be grateful.
Conceit is self-given. Be careful.

John Wooden

In creating, the only
hard thing is to
begin; a grass-blade's
no easier to make
than an oak.

James Lowe

The novelist's ambition is not to do something better than his predecessors but to see what they did not see, say what they did not say.

Milan Kundera

The man who writes about himself and his own time is the only man who writes about all people and all time.

George Bernard Shaw

No idea is so outlandish that it should not be considered with a searching but at the same time steady eye.

Winston Churchill

The role of a writer is not to say what we all can say, but what we are unable to say.

Anaïs Nin

We are apt to think that our ideas are
the creation of our own wisdom but the
truth is that they are the result of the
experience through outside contact.

Konosuke Matsushita

A story consists of someone
wanting something and
having trouble getting it.

Douglas Glover

The only difference between an artist and a lunatic is, perhaps, that the artist has the restraint or courtesy to conceal the intensity of his obsession from all except those similarly afflicted.

Osbert Sitwell

Without craft, art remains private.
Without art, craft is merely hackwork.

Joyce Carol Oates

The only joy in the world is to begin. *Cesare Pavese*

To imagine is everything, to know is nothing at all.

Anatole France

Imagination grows by exercise, and contrary to common belief, is more powerful in the mature than in the young.

W. Somerset Maugham

If there's a book you really want to read, but it hasn't been written yet, then you must write it.

Toni Morrison

Imagination is the living power and prime agent of all human perception.

Samuel Taylor Coleridge

Metaphors have a way of holding the most truth in the least space.

Orson Scott Card

Talent is a gift that brings with it an obligation to serve the world, and not ourselves, for it is not of our making.

José Martí

Literature flourishes best when it is half a trade and half an art.

William Ralph Inge

The stupid believe that to be truthful is easy, only the artist, the great artist, knows how difficult it is.

Willa Cather

Fiction is a pack of lies that masquerades as truth. Don't risk spoiling your carefully crafted lies with too much truth – or with too little.

Randy Ingermanson

What I give form to in daylight is only 1 per cent of what I have seen in darkness.

M.C. Escher

Music is the art of thinking with sounds.

Jules Combarieu

Writing has laws of perspective, of light and shade just as painting does, or music. If you are born knowing them, fine. If not, learn them. Then rearrange the rules to suit yourself.

Truman Capote

All the elements of good writing depend on the writer's skill in choosing one word instead of another.

Francine Prose

Live, travel, adventure, bless, and don't be sorry.

Jack Kerouac

When something can be read without effort, great effort has gone into its writing.

Enrique Jardiel Poncela

If I accept you as you are,
I will make you worse.
However, if I treat you as
though you are what you
are capable of becoming,
I help you become that.

Goethe

Those who do not want to imitate anything, produce nothing.

Salvador Dalí

Staying Creative

We all know the feeling: a flash of inspiration is followed by a period of exhaustion as far as creativity goes. How do we keep the tap of ideas flowing, and what can we do to free ourselves when we become stuck in the swamp of stale thinking?

When the rain falls, the creative person is excited at the prospect of seeing a rainbow.

Creativity is infinite, and the creative hunger insatiable. Don't be surprised, then, if you do not feel satisfied with the work you create. Use your dissatisfaction as the motivation to do better next time.

Fail, fail again, fail better.

Samuel Beckett

Tearing something up and throwing it away can be a positive and creative action – just so long as you are doing so in order to start again.

Your fear of failure can be defeated only by your desire to succeed.

One of the things I learned the hard way was that it doesn't pay to get discouraged. Keeping busy and making optimism a way of life can restore your faith in yourself.

Lucille Ball

Trying to please everybody is a sure way to guarantee failure: create for yourself, and use your own sense of fulfilment as the gauge for success or failure.

Adversity is sometimes necessary for creativity to flow. Many flowers need a hard frost before they bloom.

Find an inspirational quote and pin it above your workspace to motivate yourself when the going is hard.

The greater the artist, the greater the doubt. Perfect confidence is granted to the less talented as a consolation prize.

Robert Hughes

Failure is the path of least persistence.

Don't let routine become part of your problem: vary where and when you work, especially if your creative juices are not flowing.

A blank page or canvas can be intimidating. Just make a start, however, and the intimidation will melt away.

If you're not failing every now and again, it's a sign you're not doing anything very innovative.

Woody Allen

Better to have tried and failed than never to have tried at all.

If you don't feel inspired, it may be because you have cut yourself off from all sources of inspiration. Actively seeking out new experiences is the only way to ensure a steady stream of inspiration.

Did today get you nowhere? Try again tomorrow. Even Shakespeare had his off days.

When you're truly stuck, try to retrace your steps to see how you got to where you are. Is there another route you could take that would avoid your problem entirely?

Anything that is created
must sooner or later die.
Enlightenment is permanent
because we have not
produced it; we have merely
discovered it.

Chögyam Trungpa

**If you are prone to boredom,
try working on a number of
projects at the same time.**

Creative problems are as mysterious as creativity itself: often the ones that look most insurmountable turn out to be easily fixed, and those that appear minor cause us the most trouble.

Failing is of little importance
– but being content with
failure will result in never
achieving success.

The seed of your next
artwork lies embedded
in the imperfections of
your current piece.
David Bayles

It is important to develop not just creative skills, but a creative attitude too. Many people are defeated by the very prospect of the difficulties ahead, rather than the difficulties themselves.

The imagination is a fire that can never be put out by the storms of reality.

A cold shower really does wake you up when you're feeling drowsy – physically or creatively.

It's hard to make it on your own: talk to friends and colleagues when you hit a roadblock, and be prepared to listen to their advice.

It's better to fail in originality than succeed in imitation. *Herman Melville*

Ask yourself how somebody you admire would tackle the problem in front of you.

Although creative work is often hard, it is far harder to try to live with all your creative urges bottled up inside you, trying to get out.

Small errors made every single day do far more damage to your creativity than a single large error.

Don't lower your ambitions just because you fail at a project – that way can only lead into a spiral of decline. Challenge yourself constantly, and before you know it even your failures will be pretty darn good.

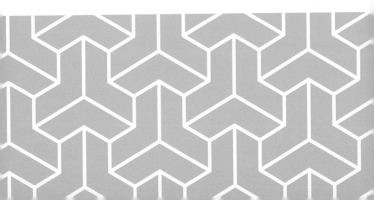

You should keep on painting no matter how difficult it is, because this is all part of experience, and the more experience you have, the better it is … unless it kills you, and then you know you have gone too far. *Alice Neel*

Often great success follows hard on the heels of a creative person's most disastrous failure.

People-watching is one way to get new fresh ideas if you are having trouble with your current idea.

You are never a failure if you are enjoying creating.

Nothing's a better cure for writer's block than to eat ice cream right out of the carton.

Don Roff

There is an old saying that when you fall off a horse you should get straight back on. Similarly, don't retire from creative work when something doesn't work out – the sooner you make a start on your next project the more quickly you will forget about earlier failings.

One way to pretty much guarantee failure tomorrow is to be blind to the faults in what you created today.

Go for a stroll with a camera, and resolve to take a certain number of pictures before you return home. Sometimes those pictures can help spark a new idea and get your creative juices flowing.

Sometimes too much encouragement by others or towards others can bring creativity and spiritual development to a standstill.

Hans Taeger

Keep a diary of what you created, how you created it and whether you were pleased with the result. When creativity seems like hard work, look back at times when you found it easy and perhaps you can find clues there as to how to open the gates of creativity once more.

This is a world for action, and not one for moping or brooding.

If you persuade yourself that you are not creative, then the ideas won't come no matter how hard you try.

Never forget your creative mistakes: study them in minute detail, for they contain a treasury of information that will help you to be more creative in the future.

Wouldn't you rather die of passion than of boredom?

Every creator painfully experiences the chasm between his inner vision and its ultimate expression.

Isaac Bashevis Singer

The truth is what is left when you have been whittled away at by the difficulties of the creative process.

Take the time to sketch out several ideas before committing yourself to one of them. If you're going to devote many hours of your life to something, you need to be sure it is an idea you fully believe in.

Open a dictionary and pick a word at random. Use that word to inspire a creative work.

It has been well said that an author who expects results from a first novel is in a position similar to that of a man who drops a rose petal down the Grand Canyon of Arizona and listens for the echo.

P.G. Wodehouse

Do not fear mistakes. In terms of creativity, there are none.

When your mind wanders, follow it – don't let it wander off without you.

Don't try to resist the mysterious force that drives you on, even if it seems to be taking you to places you don't want to go.

Our doubts are traitors, and make us lose the good we oft might win, by fearing to attempt.

William Shakespeare

Everything you experience during the creative process – both positive and negative – ultimately contributes to the finished creative work.

Ask your work what it needs, not what you need.

To be fully alive, fully human, and completely awake is to be continually thrown out of the nest.

Pema Chödrön

Each and every moment is special if we are only creative enough to recognize it as such.

It takes a while to create
something that is really good –
or even just okay. Fighting through
that tough period of mediocrity
is something that every creative
person must learn how to do.

The worst enemy to creativity is self-doubt.

We have to continually be jumping off cliffs and developing our wings on the way down. *Kurt Vonnegut*

The
Creative
Smile

Creativity is playful and joyous, not serious and sombre. In this section we celebrate the wit of creative people throughout the ages.

I'm writing a book. I've got the page numbers done.

Steven Wright

An associate producer is the only guy in Hollywood who will associate with a producer.

Fred Allen

If my doctor told me I had only six minutes to live, I wouldn't brood. I'd type a little faster.

Isaac Asimov

They called me mad, and I called them mad, and damn them they out-voted me.

Nathaniel Lee

A critic can only review the book he has read, not the one which the writer wrote.

Mignon McLaughlin

I hate reality but it's still the best place to get a good steak.

Woody Allen

I don't deserve this award, but I have arthritis and I don't deserve that either.

Jack Benny

Practically everybody in New York has half a mind to write a book, and does.

Groucho Marx

The brains of members of the press departments of motion-picture studios resemble soup at a cheap restaurant. It is wiser not to stir them.

P.G. Wodehouse

This book was written using 100 per cent recycled words.

Terry Pratchett

There's many a best-seller that could have been prevented by a good teacher.

Flannery O'Connor

I try to leave out the parts that people skip.

Elmore Leonard

Many people hear voices when
no one is there. Some of them are
called mad and are shut up in rooms
where they stare at the walls all day.
Others are called writers and they
do pretty much the same thing.

Meg Chittenden

Sex is like art. Most of it is pretty bad, and the good stuff is out of your price range.

Scott Roeben

I'm not a very good writer, but I'm an excellent rewriter.

James Michener

Said Hamlet to Ophelia, I'll draw a sketch of thee. What kind of pencil shall I use? 2B or not 2B?

Spike Milligan

You can take all the sincerity in Hollywood, place it in the navel of a fruit fly and still have room enough for three caraway seeds and a producer's heart.

Fred Allen

A critic is a man who knows the way but can't drive the car.
Kenneth Tynan

Y'know, you can't please all the people all the time . . . and last night, all those people were at my show.
Mitch Hedberg

An original idea. That can't be too hard. The library must be full of them.

Stephen Fry

The human body has two ends on it: one to create with and one to sit on. Sometimes people get their ends reversed. When this happens they need a kick in the seat of the pants.

Roger von Oech

So the writer who breeds
more words than he needs
is making a chore for the
reader who reads. *Dr. Seuss*

If you want to get rich from writing, write the
sort of thing that's read by persons who move
their lips when they're reading to themselves.

Don Marquis

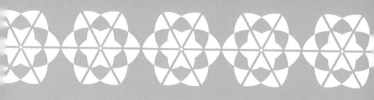

The difference between the right word and the almost right word is the difference between lightning and a lightning bug.

Mark Twain

There's a thin line between being brilliantly creative and acting like the biggest idiot on earth.

Cynthia Heimel

No author dislikes to be edited as much as he dislikes not to be published.

Russell Lynes

What is originality? Undetected plagiarism. *Dean Inge*

I never think when I write. Nobody can do two things at the same time and do them both well.

Don Marquis

You've got to learn your instrument.
Then, you practice, practice, practice.
And then, when you finally get up
there on the bandstand, forget all
that and just wail. *Charlie Parker*

Talent is cheap;
dedication is expensive.
It will cost you your life.

Irving Stone

I do not like to write –
I like to have written.

Gloria Steinem

It is easier to tone down a wild idea than
to think up a new one.

Alex Osborn

A writer is somebody for whom writing is more difficult than it is for other people.

Thomas Mann

The difference between fiction and reality? Fiction has to make sense.

Tom Clancy

I have great faith in fools – my friends call it self-confidence.

Edgar Allan Poe

If writers stopped writing about what happened to them, then there would be a lot of empty pages.

Elaine Liner

Some editors are failed writers, but so are most writers.

T.S. Eliot

There was never a genius without a tincture of madness. *Aristotle*

Asking a writer what he thinks about criticism is like asking a lamp post what it feels about dogs.

John Osborne

What is written without effort is in general read without pleasure.

Samuel Johnson

Reality is whatever refuses to go away when I stop believing in it.

Philip K. Dick

Writing is no trouble: you just jot down ideas as they occur to you. The jotting is simplicity itself – it is the occurring which is difficult.

Stephen Leacock

Art, like morality, consists in drawing the line somewhere.

G.K. Chesterton

Writing is the only profession where no one considers you ridiculous if you earn no money.

Jules Renard

It's no accident that AHA and HAHA are spelled almost the same way.

Mitch Ditkoff

If the real world were a book, it would never find a publisher. ***Jasper Fforde***

Being a writer is like having homework every night for the rest of your life.

Lawrence Kasdan

A writer is someone who can make a riddle out of an answer. *Karl Kraus*

I don't want to achieve immortality through my work. I want to achieve immortality through not dying.

Woody Allen

As my artist's statement explains, my work is utterly incomprehensible and is therefore full of deep significance.

Calvin and Hobbes

Creativity is the sudden cessation of stupidity.
Edwin H. Land

To avoid criticism, do nothing, say nothing, be nothing.
Elbert Hubbard

Humour has justly been regarded as the finest perfection of poetic genius.

Thomas Carlyle

Artists ought to walk a mile in someone else's pants. That way you're a mile away and you have their pants.

Joseph P. Blodgett

Substitute 'damn' every time you're inclined to write 'very'; your editor will delete it and the writing will be just as it should be.

Mark Twain

The holy grail is to spend less time making the picture than it takes people to look at it. *Banksy*

It was one of the dullest speeches I ever heard. The Agee woman told us for three quarters of an hour how she came to write her beastly book, when a simple apology was all that was required.

P.G. Wodehouse

Any word you have to hunt for in a thesaurus is the wrong word.

Stephen King

My favourite poem is the one that starts 'Thirty days hath September' because it actually tells you something.

Groucho Marx